CRICUT BEGINNERS

MASTER THE USE OF YOUR CRICUT MACHINE TO MAKE AMAZING AND BEAUTIFUL CRAFTS AND PROJECTS

Samuel Blade

© **Copyright 2021 - All rights reserved**.

This document is geared towards providing exact and reliable information in regard to the topic and issue covered.

- From a Declaration of Principles which was accepted and approved equally by a Committee of the American Bar Association and a Committee of Publishers and Associations.

In no way is it legal to reproduce, duplicate, or transmit any part of this document in either electronic means or in printed format. All rights reserved.

The information provided herein is stated to be truthful and consistent, in that any liability, in terms of inattention or otherwise, by any usage or abuse of any policies, processes, or directions contained within is the solitary and utter responsibility of the recipient reader. Under no circumstances will any legal responsibility or blame be held against the publisher for any reparation, damages, or monetary loss due to the information herein, either directly or indirectly.

Respective authors own all copyrights not held by the publisher.

The information herein is offered for informational purposes solely and is universal as so. The presentation of the information is without contract or any type of guarantee assurance.

The trademarks that are used are without any consent, and the publication of the trademark is without permission or backing by the trademark owner. All trademarks and brands within this book are for clarifying purposes only and are owned by the owners themselves, not affiliated with this document.

Table of Content

INTRODUCTION 13

    WHAT IS CRICUT AND WHAT IS THE PURPOSE OF CRICUT MACHINE? 13

CHAPTER 1: WHAT FUN CRAFTS CAN I DO WITH A CRICUT MACHINE? 23

    VINYL DECALS AND STICKERS 23

    FABRIC CUTS 23

    SEWING PATTERNS 24

    BALSA WOOD CUTS 24

    THICK LEATHER CUTS 24

    HOMEMADE CARDS 25

    JIGSAW PUZZLES 25

    CHRISTMAS TREE ORNAMENTS 25

    QUILTS 26

    FELT DOLLS AND SOFT TOYS 26

    T-SHIRT TRANSFERS 26

    BABY CLOTHES 27

    DOLL CLOTHES 27

    FABRIC APPLIQUÉS 27

CALLIGRAPHY SIGNS 28

JEWELRY MAKING 28

WEDDING INVITATIONS AND SAVE THE DATES 28

WEDDING MENUS, PLACE CARDS, AND FAVOR TAGS.. 29

COLORING BOOK 29

COASTERS 30

FABRIC KEYRINGS 30

HEADBANDS AND HAIR DECORATIONS 30

CUT-OUT CHRISTMAS TREE 31

CAKE TOPPERS 31

FRIDGE MAGNETS 32

WINDOW DECALS 32

SCRAPBOOKING EMBELLISHMENTS 32

CRAFT FOAM CUTS 33

BOXES AND 3D SHAPES 33

STENCILS 33

TEMPORARY TATTOOS 34

WASHI TAPE 34

ADDRESSED ENVELOPES 34

GLASSWARE DECALS 35

DECORATIONS 35

CUSHION TRANSFERS 36

GIFT TAGS 36

CLUTCH BAGS AND PURSES 36

CHAPTER 2: LATEST CRICUT MACHINES AND HOW TO CHOOSE THE BEST MACHINE FOR YOU **39**

THE CRICUT MAKER 40
CRICUT EXPLORE AIR 2 41
CRICUT EXPLORE AIR 42
CRICUT EXPLORE 1 43
WHICH MACHINE IS BETTER FOR YOU? 43

CHAPTER 3: TOOLS AND ACCESSORIES FOR CRICUT **47**

NECESSITIES 47
VINYL OR IRON-ON 52
ADDITIONAL TOOLS 56

CHAPTER 4: THE MATERIALS YOUR CRICUT MACHINE NEEDS **61**

MAIN MATERIALS 61
OTHER MATERIALS 68

CHAPTER 5: HOW WILL YOU USE YOUR CRICUT MACHINE? THE SETTING OF CRICUT MACHINE **71**

Setting up the Machine 71
Using Cricut Software 72
Imputing Cartridges and Keypad 74
Loading and Unloading Your Paper 76
Selecting Shapes, Letters, and Phrases 78
How to Remove Your Cut from the Cutting Mat 82
Techniques for Cricut Cartridges 83

CHAPTER 6: MAINTENANCE OF THE MACHINE 99

Cutting Blade 99
Subscribe to Cricut Access 101
De-tack Your Cutting Mat 101
Keep Your Cutting Mat Covers 102
Cutting Mat 102
How to Clean a Cricut Mat 103
Cleaning the Cricut Machine 104

CHAPTER 7: TIPS AND TRICKS ON HOW TO START AND HOW TO MAKE YOUR FIRST PROJECT 109

10 Top Tips and Tactics for Success 109
Cutting with Your Cricut 111

PRINT AND CUT 111
WRITING WITH YOUR CRICUT 112
SCORING WITH YOUR CRICUT 112
EMBOSSING WITH YOUR CRICUT 113
BADGES FOR YOUR CRICUT 113

CHAPTER 8: FAQ FOR CRICUT 117

WHAT IS A CRICUT? 117
WHERE CAN I DOWNLOAD THE SOFTWARE FOR THE EXPLORE MACHINES? 117
WHERE CAN I DOWNLOAD THE SOFTWARE IF I AM ON MOBILE? 118
WHAT ARE THE DIFFERENCES BETWEEN THE MACHINES? 118
DOES MY MACHINE COME WITH A CARRY BAG OF SORTS? 119
WRITING AND SCORING, CAN I DO IT? 119
IS THE DESIGN SPACE THE SAME FOR BOTH THE CRICUT MAKER AND THE EXPLORE? 119
DOES THE CRICUT MAKER HAVE FAST MODE? 120
WHAT IS THE THICKEST MY CUTTING MATERIALS CAN BE FOR THE CRICUT EXPLORE MACHINES? 120
WHAT IS THE THICKEST MY CUTTING MATERIALS CAN BE FOR THE CRICUT MAKER? 120

Do I Need the Internet? 121
Can Design Space Work on More Than One Device? 121
How Long Do Images I Have Purchased Stay in My Possession? 121
Why Is My Material Tearing All the Time and What Can I Do to Stop It? 122
Are My Old Blades Compatible with the Cricut Maker? 122
How Do I Change the Blades and Accessories? 123
Do I Need a Printer to Use My Cricut? 124

CHAPTER 9: CRICUT DICTIONARY 127

Backing 127
Bleed 127
Bonded Fabric 128
Blade 128
Blade Housing 129
Blank 129
Brayer 129
Bright Pad 129
Butcher Paper 130
Carriage 130
Cartridge 130

- Cricut Maker Adaptive Tool System 131
- Cut Lines 131
- Cutting Mat 131
- Cut Screen 131
- Drive Housing 132
- EasyPress 132
- EasyPress Mat 132
- Firmware 133
- Go Button 133
- JPG File 134
- Kiss Cut 134
- Libraries 134
- PNG File 134
- Ready to Make Projects 134
- Scraper Tool 135
- Self-Healing Mat 135
- SVG File 135
- Transfer Sheet/Paper 136
- Weeding/Reverse Weeding 136
- Weeding Tool 136

CONCLUSION 139

Introduction

What Is Cricut and What Is the Purpose of Cricut Machine?

A Cricut machine is a cutting machine. It has the unique functionality of being able to cut different materials that you will need for your crafts and DIY projects. Some of these materials include paper, vinyl, and materials as thick as wood. Although they are hardware, Cricut machines are dependent on their connection with your devices like mobile phones and computers.

Cricut machines are a very fun tool to use because they allow you to create art from materials you may not have known existed, and they allow your creativity to take flight because with the use of Cricut machines, you are able to create new materials to aid your work, and these materials you create may not be found otherwise.

In a nutshell, you create designs and templates using the device to which your machine is connected (the phone or computer system). These designs are preloaded into the device to which your Cricut is connected, and you can make a lot of changes or modifications with these designs. These designs are what you pre-load into the Cricut and use them to cut/print the material you are looking to print, just the way you want it to be.

When it comes to how a Cricut works, there is a lot to be learned about it, but having access to your own Cricut machine is like opening yourself up to a whole new world. There is literally no limit to the number of awesome crafts you can make with the use of the Cricut machine.

The Cricut machine has numerous uses besides being a shaper of structures for a scrapbook. The models themselves can be utilized to make different things, for example, welcoming cards, divider enhancements, and so much more. You have to think innovatively. There are no restrictions, and if there are, they are only an illusion of your creative mind.

Electronic cutting machines are strong instruments for specialists, educators, creators who sell their work on

Etsy, or any individual who needs to remove the unpredictable shape. You can utilize these machines to make ventures, for example, stickers, vinyl decals, custom cards, and gathering designs. They cut plans out of an assortment of materials, utilizing programming that allows you to transfer, make, or buy drawings to be cut. Also, frequently, in the event that you put in a pen rather than a cutting edge, they can draw as well. A snappy voyage through Instagram hashtags demonstrates the full scope of activities individuals make with these machines.

Remember that these machines have an expectation to learn and adapt, particularly with the product. Many people have heard of a Cricut machine and it's been making a big splash in the crafting world because of everything that you can do with it. You might be surprised that you would be able to work with this machine with a lot of different materials and it can be a really fun way to make some great items.

When Cricut machines first came out, you needed cartridges to be able to cut out your letters and the shapes that you want to use for your items but now, you don't need cartridges at all! Now everything is done digitally because everyone understands that we have great technology at our feet, and we should use it to our advantage.

Most Cricut machines will now work over Bluetooth or Wi-Fi as well, which means that you can use your iPad or if you have an iPhone, you can use this as well. You can also use this from your computer. This makes designing your passions easier than ever and you have a complete versatility that will help you be able to do what you want and have creative options for you.

All machines come with the following items:

- Practice project materials
- A power adapter
- A cutting machine
- Access to free projects that are ready to make
- A cutting mat that is twelve inches by twelve inches
- A USB cable

- A free membership (it's only a trial one) to access to Cricut
- Guide for making setup easy
- Fine point blade (that is premium) and housing for the blade

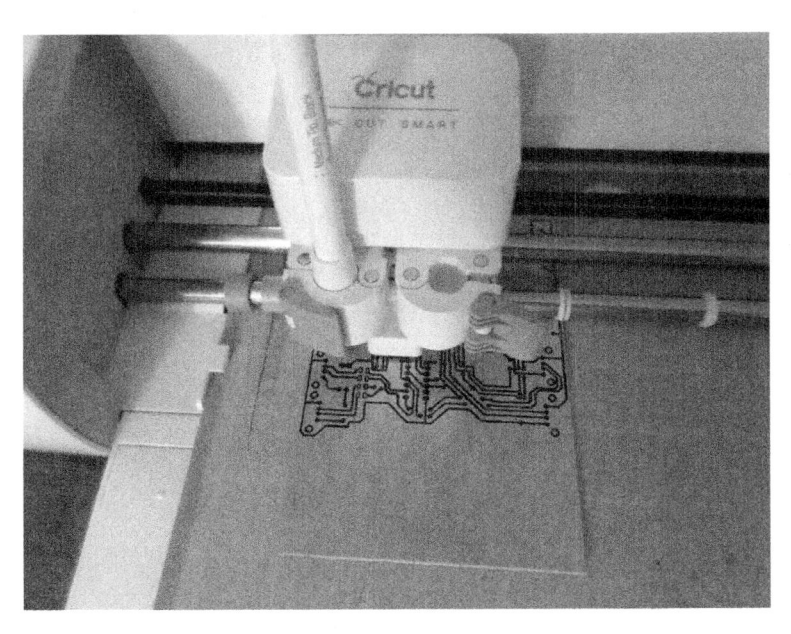

Another thing that you should know is that certain models come with additional items such as a specialized writing pen, different blades or even wheels.

A Cricut machine is a cutting machine. Specifically, it is known as a die-cutting machine. You can use it for paper crafting along with other crafting supplies as well.

It's a machine that boasts of being excellent at crafting with precision. Many people think that these machines just cut paper, but they cut so much more than that.

Every machine will have its own software that is with its brand. It will be free to use and to download into or onto your machine. Cricut even has an app you can use. The app is friendly to the user and you are able to upload images and create designs. You can make your designs from scratch or purchase the designs from others. You can also upload images and purchase designs from the application and modify them to your custom designs.

The app is extremely easy to use and the software is very simple while being user-friendly as well. It gives you the freedom to have creativity with your projects. What you make in this will tell your machine where it needs to score or write. It also tells us where to cut.

If there is just one step, the machine can do a full design. However, if there are multiple steps, then your machine will convey this to you through the device that you have connected to it. It will tell you if you have additional steps as well.

A machine like this isn't necessarily a printer, though it can be said that it comes close. If you use the Print then Cut method it will let you have any design for your project, and it will take it from there for you to be able to use it properly. If you want to think about this easily, it would be a little like making stickers.

It also cuts more than paper. These machines are not just for die-hard scrapbookers anymore. It cuts so much more than that. As such, this book will include a master list of everything that will work with your machine and how to gain the most benefit from it.

Close your machine when you're not utilizing it to dodge residue subsiding into the cutting region. Wipe any residue or paper garbage away from the sharp edge and cutting zone with a perfect, dry material, yet simply after you've unplugged the machine.

The cutting mats for the majority of the machines accompany a plastic film to cover the glue side. Clutch these to expand the life of your cutting mats. You can likewise draw out your tangle's life by scratching ceaselessly any bits of material left on it after an undertaking utilizing a spatula device. When the adhesiveness has gone, you'll need to supplant the mats. You can discover stunts to invigorate the floor coverings, yet we've never attempted them.

Chapter 1: What Fun Crafts Can I Do with a Cricut Machine?

Vinyl Decals and Stickers

One of the projects you can carry out with the Cricut Maker is cutting vinyl and stickers.

You just have to create your design in Cricut Design Space, instruct the Maker to cut, then weed and transfer the design to whatever surface you choose.

Fabric Cuts

The presence of the Rotary Blade in the Cricut Maker makes it a well-respected machine. The Maker can cut any type of fabric, including chiffon, denim, silk and even heavy canvas. With this machine, you can definitely cut huge amounts of fabrics without using any backup, and this is because it comes equipped with a fabric cutting mat. Awesome machine!

Sewing Patterns

One major benefit of owning the Cricut Maker machine is the extensive library of sewing patterns that you'll have access to.

The library has hundreds of patterns, including some from Riley Blake Designs and Simplicity; all you need to do is select the pattern you want and the machine will do the cutting.

Balsa Wood Cuts

The knife blade, coupled with the 4 kg force of the machine, means that the Cricut Maker can easily cut through thick materials (up to 2.4 mm thick). With these features, thick materials that were off-limits for earlier Cricut machines are now being done.

Thick Leather Cuts

Just like balsa wood, the Cricut Maker is also used for thick leather cuts.

Homemade Cards

Paper crafters use the Cricut Maker because the power and precision of the machine make the cutting of cards and paper far quicker and easier. With the machine, homemade cards just got better.

Jigsaw Puzzles

With the Cricut Maker, crafters can make jigsaw puzzles because the knife blade cuts through much thicker materials than ever before.

Christmas Tree Ornaments

Cricut machine owners can easily make Christmas tree ornaments. All you have to do is go through the sewing library for Christmas patterns, use any fabric of your choice to cut out the pattern, and sew them together. Remember, the rotary blade cuts through all sorts of fabric.

Quilts

Thanks to the partnership between Cricut and Riley Blake Designs, Cricut Design Space now has a number of quilting patterns in the sewing pattern gallery.

The Cricut Maker is now used to cut quilting pieces with high precision before they are sewn together.

Felt Dolls and Soft Toys

The "felt dolls and clothes" pattern is one of the simplest designs in the sewing pattern library. Thus, it is used for homemade dolls and toys.

The process is easy; just select the pattern you want, cut, and then sew.

T-shirt Transfers

The Cricut Maker is used for cutting out heat transfer vinyl for crafters to transfer their designs to fabric. To achieve this, you have to make your design in Design Space, load the machine with your heat transfer vinyl, cut the material, and then iron the transfer onto the T-shirt. Alternatively, you can use the Cricut EasyPress to transfer the vinyl.

Baby Clothes

The Cricut Maker cannot cut adult clothing patterns because the mat size is only 12" x 24". However, you can easily make baby clothing patterns with the machine.

Doll Clothes

Just like baby clothes, the Cricut Maker can easily make doll clothing patterns because the mat size is big enough.

Fabric Appliqués

The bonded fabric blade doesn't come with the Cricut Maker, but if you buy it, you will be able to use your machine to cut complex fabric designs like appliqué. For the bonded fabric blade to cut effectively, there has to be bonded backing on the material.

Calligraphy Signs

The stand-out feature of the Cricut Maker is the Adaptive Tool System. With this feature, the machine will remain relevant in the foreseeable future because it fits with all the blades and tools of the explore series, as well as all future blades and tools made by Cricut.

The calligraphy pen is one of such tools, and it is ideal for sign and card making.

Jewelry Making

For crafters that like to explore jewelry making, the power of the Cricut Maker means that you can cut thicker materials, and while you can't cut things like diamonds, silver, or gold, you can definitely try to make a beautiful pair of leather earrings.

Wedding Invitations and Save the Dates

Weddings are capital intensive, and we all know how the so-called 'little' expenses, like save the dates and invitations, can add up to the huge cost. However, if you have the Cricut Maker machine, then you can make your invitations and save the dates yourself.

The Maker is capable of making invitations of the highest quality. It cuts out intricate paper designs and the calligraphy pen is very useful too.

Wedding Menus, Place Cards, and Favor Tags

The Cricut Maker is not restricted to the production of pre-wedding invitations and save the dates. With the machine, you can also produce other items such as place cards, wedding menus, favor tags, etc.

In order to keep the theme front and center, the crafter is advised to use a similar design for all their stationery.

Coloring Book

With the Cricut Maker, you can make 'mindful coloring' books from scratch. To achieve this goal, you need a beautiful design, a card, and paper. Then you command the Cricut Maker to create your personal and completely unique coloring book with the aid of the fine-point pen tool.

Coasters

In the sewing library, there are a number of beautiful coaster patterns and as such, the Maker is used to coasters.

With the Cricut Machine, you can work with materials such as metallic sheets, quilt, leather, and everything in between.

Fabric Keyrings

The Cricut Maker makes fabric keyrings and the process is simple—it cuts out the pattern and then sews it together. Besides, there are a number of designs for fabric keyrings in the sewing pattern library.

Headbands and Hair Decorations

The Cricut Maker is known to cut through materials like thick leather and this has gone on to inspire the production of intricate headbands and hair decorations. The machine is so inspiring; crafters in the fashion world use it for creative designs and projects.

Cut-Out Christmas Tree

It is a normal tradition for people to buy Christmas trees during the holiday season. However, if you don't have enough space for a big tree in your living room, or maybe you're allergic to pine, then you can definitely create your own Christmas tree.

The production of an interlocking wooden tree is something the Cricut Maker does easily because the blade is capable of cutting through thick materials like wood. With the Cricut Maker, you don't use a laser.

Cake Toppers

When Cricut bought over the cake cutter machine, the idea was to create shapes made of gum paste, fondant, and others.

It is obvious that the Cricut Maker can't cut as good as the cake machine; however, it can be used to produce tiny and intricate paper designs that can be used to decorate cakes.

Fridge Magnets

Cricut machines like the Maker and Explore Air are capable of cutting out magnetic materials. Thus, crafters can use the Maker to make those fancy magnetic designs placed on refrigerators.

Window Decals

If you're one of those who love to display inspiring quotes on your windows or even fancy little patterns on your car, then the Maker got you covered.

You just have to load the Maker with window cling and get your design created.

Scrapbooking Embellishments

The Cricut Maker is used for embellishments when scrapbooking. It is public knowledge that Cricut machines are super when it comes to cutting intricate designs. However, the Cricut Maker takes it to a whole new level, and the responsive new blades take away all forms of complexity.

Craft Foam Cuts

In the past, Cricut machines found it difficult to cut craft foam (especially the Explore machines); however, the Cricut Maker, with the 4 kg of force, cuts through craft foam very easily.

Boxes and 3D Shapes

The Cricut machines come with a scoring stylus and this tool can create items with the sharpest edges imaginable.

We all know that the Cricut Maker can execute all kinds of sewing patterns thrown at it. It can also cut paper crafts, including 3D shapes and boxes.

Stencils

The Maker comes in handy for people that create things that are used to create other items. The machine is incredible for making stencils, bearing in mind that you can utilize thicker materials to create the stencils.

Temporary Tattoos

If you're one of those people that want to have tattoos, but don't want them permanent for life, then the Cricut Maker is your go-to machine.

With the Cricut Maker, you can etch your design on a tattoo paper (mostly coated with transfer film) and use it on your skin.

Washi Tape

Crafters that use Washi tape for scrapbooking can testify how expensive it can be, especially when buying bulk from craft stores. However, those who own the Cricut machine can use it to cut out Washi sheets—they can print-and-cut their personal designs on it.

Addressed Envelopes

The Cricut Maker is an astounding machine that can save you from spending on certain items. Remember, we talked about making handmade wedding invitations; with the Cricut Machine, you can also make envelopes to go with the cards. Another good feature about the machine is that it is equipped with a calligraphy pen and a fine-point pen, meaning that it is capable of addressing your envelopes automatically. All you need to do is make sure that the words are clear enough for the postman to read.

Glassware Decals

With a Cricut Maker, you can cut vinyl to make glassware designs. People who host themed parties will love this one, e.g., if you're hosting a summer house party and you're serving mojitos, you can decorate your drinking glasses with coconuts and palm tree decals. Also, people holding Xmas parties can design and cut themed stickers to use on their cups.

Decorations

There are a couple of other desktop craft machines that are used to create general household decorations, but the Cricut Maker is one of the best—if not the very best.

With the Cricut Maker, you'll be empowered to create 3D wall hangings, beautiful cut-outs in the living room, and even things like signage in your closets, etc.

Cushion Transfers

With your Cricut Maker, you can brighten up your cushion and pillows by adding your homemade designs. With the flocked iron-on vinyl, you can create a lovely textured cushion using heat transfer vinyl on the Cricut machine.

Gift Tags

We all know that gift tags consume some of our money during the holiday season. However, with your Cricut Maker, you don't have to buy them anymore; you can just make your own.

Clutch Bags and Purses

The sewing pattern library is awesome; thus you can make different types of full-size purses, coin purses and even clutch bags.

Chapter 2: Latest Cricut Machines and How to Choose the Best Machine for You

This is definitely the most important thing that comes to your mind while you learn everything about the Cricut Machine.

Buying the best Cricut machine would complement your creativity and would help you create crafts, designs, projects, and ornaments. First of all, what you need to know about buying Cricut machines is that all Cricut machines work in the same way.

The thing that sets them apart or creates a difference in the Cricut machine is the unique features that are designated to them.

The similarity that every Cricut machine has is that each machine uses a free software called Design Space.

It is important to know that every cutting machine has its own software, which is difficult to learn.

The most interesting thing about Cricut is that it is easier and more straightforward to use and create interesting things. You can download Design Craft and start using it even before you buy a Cricut machine. This would give you a good handle on Design Space, and you would be able to make things easier. If we are going to classify Cricut machines based on their features, then it would be as follows:

The Cricut Maker

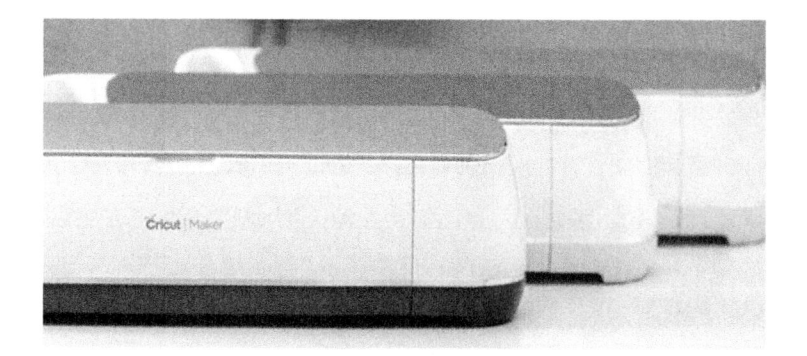

It is the most recent type of cutting machine that has yet to be released. Its specialty lies in its ability to cut wood and fabrics. The Cricut Maker is the only machine that has a rotary cutter for fabrics and crepe paper. To cut thick materials like wood, foam board, etc., Cricut Maker has now a knife blade installed in it that makes the wood cutting easier and better. The rotary cutter comes along with the packing of the Cricut Maker. But you will have to buy the knife blade separately. If you wish to change or switch different cutting tools, then you have to undo the clamp on side "B." After you have opened the clamp, put the tool of your choice and then close it. All this tells about how Cricut Maker is recently the best and extremely convenient to use.

Cricut Explore Air 2

Cricut Explore Air 2 is a diminution to the Cricut Maker. Although it is not compatible with the knife blade or rotary cutter, it can still cut hundreds of materials. It is better in a way that it cuts things twice faster than a

Cricut Explore Air does. It is also cheaper than the Cricut Maker, usually less than half of the price.

Cricut Explore Air

It functions almost similar to Cricut Explore Air 2. The only difference is that this machine cuts a bit slower. As compared to Cricut Explore Air 2, the project thus takes time to finish.

Their prices are also almost the same.

That is why I would suggest you choose Cricut Explore Air 2 if you are facing difficulty in affording the Cricut Maker. It also has a Bluetooth embedded for wireless connections, making it convenient for Apple and Android users to feel the need to use the computer while using this machine.

Cricut Explore 1

Cricut Explore 1 is again a diminution to Cricut Explore Air. It is the first-ever Cricut machine that eliminated the need to use cartridges and introduced the internet Design Space feature allowing you to make designs and projects of your choice. The drawback that it has is that it does not have Bluetooth, so you need to attach a computer directly to it.

Otherwise, it would not work.

Which Machine Is Better for You?

With that being said, if you are looking for a Cricut machine at a reasonable price, then I would recommend you to buy Cricut Explore Air 2. It would also be easy to use if you are a beginner. But if you have enough budget, then Cricut Maker would definitely be the best option.

Chapter 3: Tools and Accessories for Cricut

You can't possibly use a Cricut machine alone, but the type of accessories or tools that you need depends on the kind of project that you're using the machine for. If you're going into home décor, you'll need different tools from those going into paper crafts.

Necessities

Irrespective of any project, some necessary accessories are essential. Some of these accessories come with Cricut, while some can be purchased from Cricut.

- **Cutting Mats**

Cutting mats come in three kinds, which are strong grip, standard grip, and light grip. You can also purchase any one of the sizes that they come in, which is either the 12 inches by 24 inches or the 12 inches by 12 inches mat.

The strong grip mat is ideal when you're cutting stiffened fabric, glitter cardstock, chipboard, specialty cardstock, and other thick materials. For thinner materials like embossed cardstock or standard cardstock, vinyl, pattern paper, or iron-on, we recommend the standard grip mat. For the lightest materials, a light grip mat is needed. Light materials include light cardstock, office paper, vellum, or other materials.

A newly bought Cricut machine includes a cutting mat in the box, and so you don't have to buy a mat separately. After a while, the mat will lose its stickiness and you can either apply glue to maintain it or buy a new one.

Also, when considering your project, you should get the right mat. If your mat is light grip and you try to cut a thick fabric, you might end up messing the entire project up because the material will keep on shifting from the mat.

- **Cutting Blades**

Cutting Blades are the essential accessories needed when using Cricut. After all, you can't cut without a blade.

Cutting blades also come in three types. First, we have the standard blade that usually accompanies the Cricut machine. The blade is very sharp and strong, but after a while, you will need to change the blade when it becomes blunt. So, you should have extra blades on hand just in case.

Next, we have the German carbide blade. You can easily purchase this from Cricut too. It's stronger than the standard blade, and it is created to cut through mid-weight materials. The blade also lasts for a longer time and doesn't easily break.

Lastly, designed for very thick materials, we have the deep-cut blade. The deep-cut blade is meant for cutting materials that go with the strong grip cutting mat. You can also use the blade to cut materials like stamp material, magnet, and some other fabrics.

- **Spatula and Scraper**

Not many people bother with purchasing a spatula and scraper when they want to use their Cricut machine. But these tools are useful when it comes to taking materials off the cutting mat.

For the spatula, you can use it to remove the material from the mat without damaging the material. It provides accuracy. In the case of the scraper, you will need to maintain the mat by cleaning it. This tool is helpful with scraping off leftover materials on the mat and cleaning it. This keeps the machine durable and it will last for a long time. Also, when you want to start a new project, you can quickly use the mat without having to clean it.

Apart from these essential tools, for specific types of projects, some devices are crucial when working on those projects.

Vinyl or Iron-On

For example, when working on vinyl or iron-on projects, they both use the same type of tools because they are both similar. Iron-on plans are pretty much heat transfer vinyl projects.

You can use vinyl to decorate tumblers, cups, or mugs; create decals for frames or walls and other projects. Iron-on is used to decorate fabric like adding designs on t-shirts.

- **Transfer Tape**

Cricut also manufactures this tool and it is entirely transparent. This way, when transferring or placing your vinyl project, you can see it easily and handle it more carefully.

- **Weeder**

When carrying out vinyl or iron-on projects, a weeder is crucial because it can be used to single out tiny pieces that are on your project like the pieces of vinyl that aren't being used from the backing sheet.

- **Paper**

Apart from vinyl projects, paper projects are probably the most popular projects that most crafters carry out. When using Cricut, most people start with paper projects because they are light and relatively more comfortable to do.

You can use paper to create shapes, numbers, letters, cards, envelopes, banners, decorations, stickers, and more. For paper projects, there are two general tools that you will possibly need.

- **Pens**

When using any of the Cricut Explore machines, you can quickly write out your designs. When you want to draw, Cricut provides some free fonts and some fonts that you can buy from Cricut Access. Also, if you have fonts on your computer, you can use that too.

You can buy different pens from Cricut that are compatible with any of the Explore machines. Their types of pens include calligraphy pens, fine tip pens, gold pens, metallic pens, and pens of a wide range of colors. Although you can use other pens, Cricut machines work best with Cricut pens.

The great thing about Cricut machines is that they provide two slots so that you can use the pen and the blade simultaneously. This allows for quick designing and cutting instantaneously.

- **Scoring Tool**

This is also called a scoring stylus, and it is used for folding lines on boxes, envelopes, cards or any other paper. In the same way that you can design or draw and cut at the same time, you can also install the scoring tool in the machine when the blade is already installed.

This makes your designing process fast and easy.

Additional Tools

Apart from the usual design tools, you can also purchase some tools that make using the Cricut machine more convenient. Depending on the project you are using, these tools might be handy.

- **Tool Kit**

Instead of purchasing your tools one-by-one, some people go for the economical option and buy a tool kit. A standard tool kit should include scissors, weeders, scrapers, spatulas, and tweezers. If you're going into iron-on or vinyl projects, then you should probably purchase this type of tool kit.

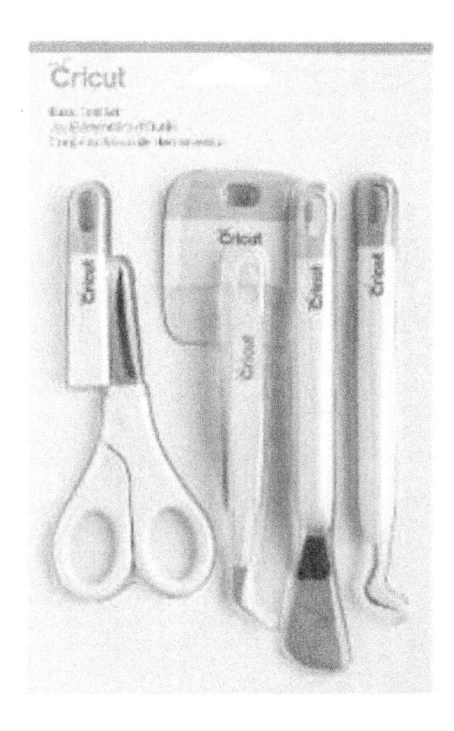

Some advanced tool kits add a paper trimmer and scoring stylus. This tool kit is excellent for those interested in paper projects.

- **Bluetooth Adapter**

Cricut Explore 1 does not come with an inbuilt Bluetooth adapter. If you want to use this model, you can buy a Bluetooth adapter from Cricut. This way, you can easily use your Cricut wherever your computer, laptop, or iPad is.

Chapter 4: The Materials Your Cricut Machine Needs

There are hundreds of different materials that can be worked on with Cricut machines. To be precise, Cricut machines can cut through many materials that are precisely or below 2.0 millimeters thickness. Users with Cricut Maker models have more cutting force and size advantage. The Cricut Maker model cuts ten times faster and can put up with materials that are up to 2.4 millimeters in thickness.

Many materials can be cut with a Cricut machine, even though the machine is mostly known for cutting paper or vinyl. The type of material to use depends solely on the type of objects you want to work with.

Main Materials

The type of materials you will choose for your cut will significantly depend on the kind of projects you want to engage in. Some of these materials work with different blades and can be used with more than one

Cricut blade—this makes them be the essential materials associated with Cricut cutting and are the primary materials for your Cricut Explore machine.

To be more organized, we will mention some of them by category. You may be familiar with some of them as a beginner. However, you can pick up new materials from these categories and start trying them out on new projects.

Paper and Cardstock

It seems somewhat necessary to start with this category because they are the most popularly used class of material when designing. They have over thirty-five different kinds of materials under them, therefore making them the category with the highest number of resources.

Paper is another primary material you can use for cutting. You can make homemade greeting cards and envelopes from cutting paper with different designs. You can always choose from various types of paper from corrugated cardboard, kraft paper, foil, glitter paper, and many more.

Types of Paper or Cardboard

- Construction paper
- Cardstock
- Kraft board
- Metallic paper
- Copy paper

Transfer Tape

This is a clear, medium-strength adhesive tape that comes in sheets. This is an absolutely invaluable step of the process. We have some tips for you on getting the most out of your transfer tape and on choosing a transfer tape that will come in a quantity and power that is right for you and your projects.

I will tell you that the Cricut brand transfer tape comes in a single, rolled 12" x 48" sheet. You can cut pieces to your liking and use them multiple times before disposing of them. These sheets from Cricut are currently $8.99 at a local crafting retailer, while other brands offer a 12" roll of six to ten feet for a similar price.

While transfer tape is an absolutely integral part of the process of using your Cricut machine, the brand is not that important. Do some shopping around, find a sample size that works for you and your price point, and get started!

Like with any new type of crafting project, it will take some time to get used to the supplies and products, and to find the things that really work the best for you.

Now that a lot has been said about different types of materials that can be used on Cricut machines; you should be getting inspired to try out new different projects with these materials. However, only a beginner would stop here. We're not even close to unfolding the amazing parts of the usage of Cricut machines. You will get to know much later on in this book about the capabilities of Cricut machines and what you can do with them on an advanced level. Buckle up!

Vinyl

Professionals use vinyl materials a lot because they find them very effective and outstanding for making graphics, stencils, decals, signs, and so on. There are about 11 materials made from vinyl that can be used on Cricut machines.

Iron-On

This is also a vinyl product, but with a different framework. You can make use of this type of vinyl to design and decorate tote bags, t-shirts, caps, and other clothing items. There are around 9 iron-on materials that are used on Cricut machines.

Iron-on vinyl is also called heat transfer vinyl and one of the treasured materials to cut with Cricut Explore Air 2. You can use the iron-on vinyl to design bags, t-shirts, and any other items.

Types of Iron-on

- Printable iron-on
- Glossy iron-on
- Metallic iron-on
- Foil iron-on

Fabric and Textiles

Fabrics are naturals on Cricut machines; they work seamlessly on almost every Cricut machine model. There are about 17 different materials under this category. However, most of the time, they need stabilizers to be added before cutting.

Textile or Fabric is not an unusual material for some Cricut users, but because the variety of fabric available to choose from is so vast, it needs to be mentioned again because there are some techniques and materials that are a little more unusual. For example, cutting a lace-like pattern into fabrics can immediately add a color palette of fancy lace to any project. This also makes it possible to have the same lace pattern on a variety of complimentary fabrics or colors.

There is a fabric blade that is specific to the fabric material; all you need to do is to keep the fabric set in place on the settings dial. Cricut has some fabric materials online that you can cut with.

Types of Fabric

- Leather
- Canvas
- Duck cloth
- Silk
- Linen

Infusible Ink

Infusible ink is an exciting material from Cricut that allows heat transfer on white and light-colored materials. It comes in different colors, patterns, and gradients and is designed to be resistant to peeling, flaking and washing. It can be used for shirts, totes, coasters, etc.

Other Materials

Apart from all these five categories of materials we have discussed, there are several other unique materials that can also be used on Cricut machines. Ranging from by-products of foils, woods, sheets, board, Bellum, chips, tapes to many other natural and artificial resources, there are at least 30 of them that can be worked on by Cricut machines. There are materials that people think are not compatible with Cricut machines. Well, you'd be surprised.

Faux Leather and Leather

Depending on your preference, you can use either material. Despite what you choose, both are good materials to cut with the Cricut. Custom jewelry, like necklace pendants or earrings, is simple and stunning projects. These make beautiful and personal gifts or add the right touch to a special outfit. Leather can also be used for making fashionable bracelets or cuffs.

Having an intricate cut on a lovely piece of leather or faux leather, the bracelet can be attached to an adjustable band. Hair bows or bows to add to clothing or handbags are also possible. For a hair bow, glue a hair clip to the back when the bow is finished. Use hot glue or another adhesive to attach the bow to clothing or a purse. Other hair accessories can be made, like flowers and other shapes.

These can be attached to hair clips, like the bows, or attached to hard or stretchy headbands. Leather can also be used as an embellishment to pillows or other fabrics, like chair backs, or made into manly coasters.

Felt

Felt is another multi-functional material that you can use for a host of projects. Because this item is fairly sturdy but has good flexibility, it is perfect for just about anything.

In addition, it comes in all different colors and is relatively inexpensive. Some unique projects that can be made from felt include garlands of multi-layered flowers to hang over a window curtain or above a bed, a textured phrase attached to a pillow, an interactive tree-shaped advent calendar, banners, ornaments, and cupcake or cake toppers.

Chapter 5: How Will You Use Your Cricut Machine? The Setting of Cricut Machine

So, you have all your materials on hand, which is awesome, but how do you actually use a Cricut machine? Well, that's what you're about to find out. If looking at your Cricut machine makes you feel confused, then continue reading—here, we'll tell you how to use your new Cricut machine in a simple, yet effective way.

Setting up the Machine

First, you'll want to set up the Cricut machine. To begin, create a space for it. A craft room is the best place for this, but if you're at a loss of where to put it, I suggest setting it up in a dining room if possible. Make sure you have an outlet nearby or a reliable extension cord.

Next, read the instructions. Often, you can jump right in and begin using the equipment, but with Cricut machines, it can be very tedious. The best thing to do is to read all the materials you get with your machine.

Make sure that you do have ample free space around the machine itself, because you will be loading mats in and out and you'll need that little bit of wiggle room.

The next thing to set up is, of course, the computer where the designs will be created. Make sure that whatever medium you're using has an internet connection, since you'll need to download the Cricut Design Space app. If it's a machine earlier than the Explore Air 2, it will need to be plugged in directly, but if it's a wireless machine like the Air 2, you can simply link this up to your computer, and from there, design what you need to design.

Using Cricut Software

So, Cricut machines use a program called Cricut Design Space, and you'll need to make sure that you have this downloaded and installed when you're ready. Download the app if you plan to use a smartphone or tablet, or if you're on the computer, go to http://design.cricut.com/setup to get the software. If it's not hooked up already, make sure you've got Bluetooth compatibility enabled on the device, or the cord plugged in. To turn on your machine, hold the power button. You'll then go to settings, where you should see your Cricut model in Bluetooth settings. Choose that, and from there, your device will ask you to put a Bluetooth passcode in. Just make this something generic and easy to remember.

Once that's done, you can now use Design Space.

So, what I love about Design Space is that it's incredibly easy to use. They know you're a beginner, so you'll notice it's very easy to navigate.

Now, I personally like to use the app for Design Space, since this will allow you to have every design uploaded to the cloud so that you can reuse your designs. However, if you want to use them without having an internet connection, you'll want to make sure that you download them and save them to the device itself, rather than relying on the cloud.

When you're in the online mode, you'll see a lot of projects that you can use. For the purpose of this tutorial, I do suggest making sure that you choose an easy one, such as the "Enjoy Card" project you can get automatically.

So, you've got everything linked up—let's move onto the first cut for this project.

Imputing Cartridges and Keypad

The first cut that you'll be doing involves keypad input and cartridges, and these are usually done with the "Enjoy Card" project you get right away. So, once everything is set up, choose this project, and from there, you can use the tools and the accessories within the project.

You will need to set the smart dial before you get started making your projects. This is on the right side of the Explore Air 2, and it's basically the way you choose your materials. Turn the dial to whatever type of material you want, since this helps with ensuring you've got the right blade settings. There are even half settings for those in-between projects.

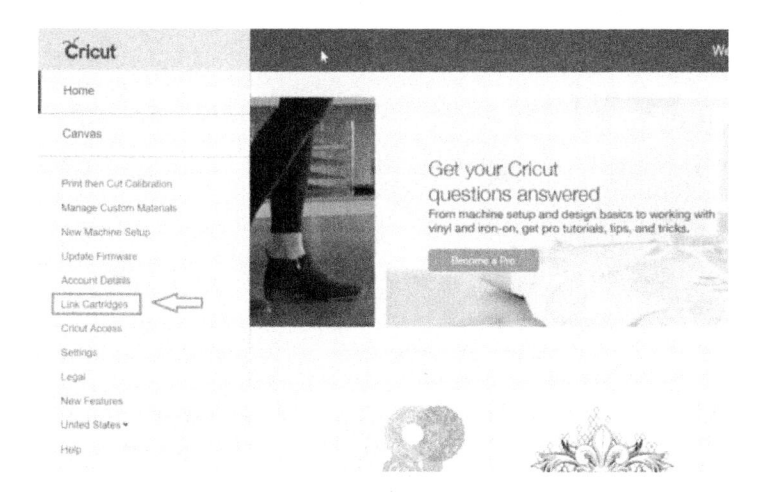

For example, let's say you have some light cardstock. You can choose that setting, or the adjacent half setting. Once this is chosen in Design Space, your machine will automatically adjust to the correct setting.

You can also choose the fast mode, which is in the "set, load, go" area on the screen, and you can then check the position of the box under the indicator for dial position. Then, press this and make your cut. However, the fast mode is incredibly loud, so be careful.

Now, we've mentioned cartridges. While these usually aren't used in the Explore Air 2 machines anymore, they are helpful with beginner projects. To do this, once you have the Design Space software and everything is

75

connected, go to the hamburger menu and you'll see an option called "ink cartridges." Press that bad boy, and from there, choose the Cricut device. The machine will then tell you to put your cartridge in. Do that, and once it's detected, it will tell you to link the cartridge.

Remember, though, that once you link this, you can't use it with other machines—the one limit to these cartridges.

Once it's confirmed, you can go to images, and click the cartridges option to find the ones that you want to make. You can filter the cartridges to figure out what you need, and you can check out your images tab for any other cartridges that are purchased or uploaded.

You can get digital cartridges, which means you buy them online and choose the images directly from your available options. They aren't physical, so there is no linking required.

Loading and Unloading Your Paper

To load paper into a Cricut machine, you'll want to make sure that the paper is at least three inches by three inches. Otherwise, it won't cut very well. You should use regular paper for this.

Now, to make this work, you need to put the paper onto the cutting mat. You should have one of those, so take it right now and remove the attached film. Put a corner of the paper to the area where you are directed to align the paper corners. From there, push the paper directly onto the cutting mat for proper adherence. Once you do that, you just load it into the machine, following the arrows. You'll want to keep the paper firmly on the mat. Press the "load paper" key that you see as you do this. If it doesn't take for some reason, press the unload paper key, and try this again until it shows up.

Now, before you do any cutting for your design, you should always have a test cut in place. Some people don't do this, but it's incredibly helpful when learning how to use a Cricut. Otherwise, you won't get the correct pressure in some cases, so get in the habit of doing it for your pieces.

Is there a difference between vinyl and other products? The primary difference is the cutting mats. Depending on what you're cutting, you may need some grip or lack thereof. If you feel like your material isn't fully sticking, get some Heat N' Bond to help with this since often the issue with cutting fabrics comes from the fact that it doesn't adhere. But you may also need mats that are a bit thicker, too, to help get a better grip on these.

Selecting Shapes, Letters, and Phrases

When you're creating your design in Design Space, you usually begin by using letters, shapes, numbers, or different fonts. These are the basics and they're incredibly easy.

To make text, you just press the text tool on the left-hand side and type out your text. For example, write the word hello, or joy, or whatever you want to use.

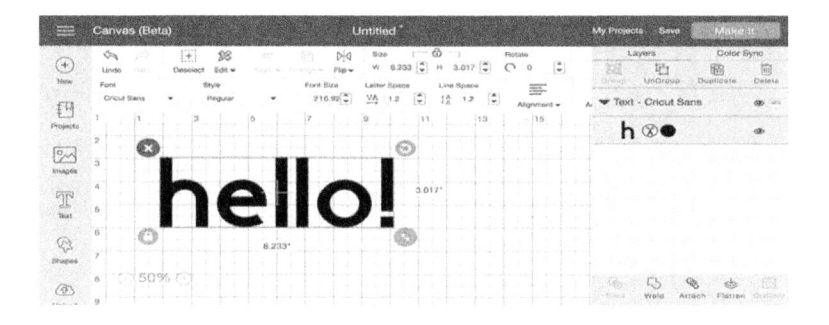

You can change the font size by pressing the drag and drop arrow near the corner of the text box, or by going to the size panel near the top to choose actual font sizes. You can also choose different Cricut or system fonts, too. Cricut ones will be in green, and if you have Cricut Access, this is a great way to begin using this. You can also sort them, so you don't end up accidentally paying for a font.

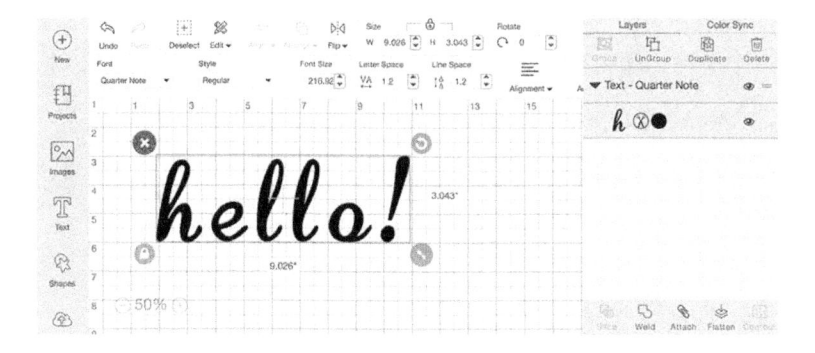

The Cricut ones are supposed to be made for Cricut, so you know they'll look good. Design Space also lets you

79

put them closer together so they can be cut with a singular cut. You can change this by going to line spacing and adjusting as needed. To fix certain letters, you go to the drop-down advanced menu to ungroup the letters, so everything is separate as needed.

Cricut also offers different writing styles, which is a great way to add text to projects. The way to do this is to choose a font that's made with a specific style and choose only the Cricut ones, and then go to writing. This will then narrow down the choice so you're using a good font for writing.

Adding shapes is pretty easy, as well. In Design Space, choose the shapes option. Once you click it, the window will then pop out, and you'll have a wonderful array of different shapes that you can use with just one click. Choose your shape, and from there, put it in the space. Drag the corners in order to make this bigger or smaller.

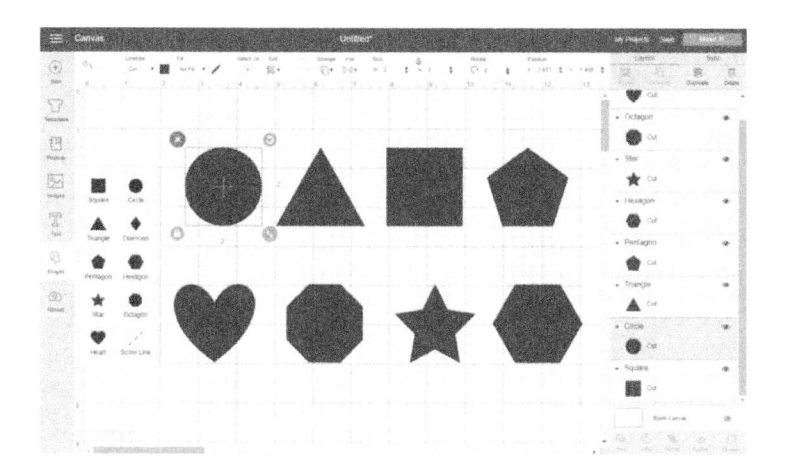

There is also the scoreline, which creates a folding line for you to use. Personally, if you're thinking of trying to make a card at first, I suggest using this.

You can also resize your options by dragging them towards the right-hand side, and you can change the orientation by choosing that option and then flipping it around. You can select exact measurements as well, which is good for those design projects that need everything to be precise.

Once you've chosen the design, it's time for you to start cutting, and we'll discuss this next step below.

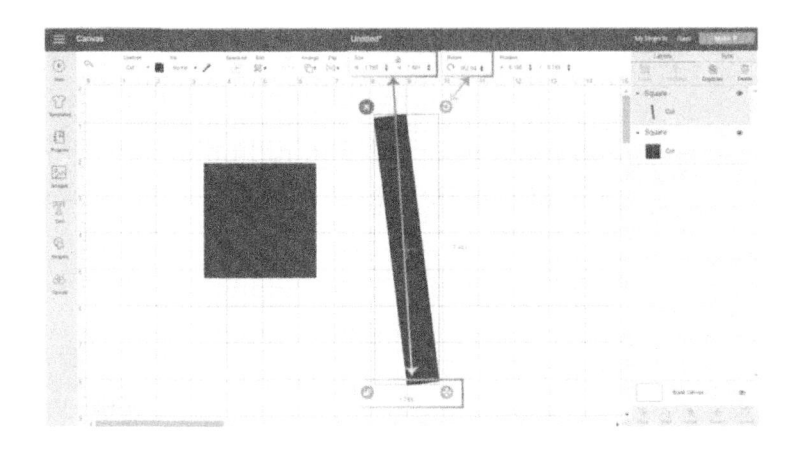

How to Remove Your Cut from the Cutting Mat

Removing your cut from the mat is easy, but complicated. Personally, I ran into the issue of it being more complicated with vinyl projects since they love to just stick around there. But we'll explain how you can create great cuts and remove them, as well.

Techniques for Cricut Cartridges

On the off chance that you've been a piece of the general Cricut fever that keeps on clearing the country, at that point you've without a doubt been satisfied that you're never again compelled to pay the first high costs as when Cricut cartridges were at first discharged. The Lite Cupcake Wrappers cartridge isn't a special case to this standard.

The Cupcake Wrappers Cartridge Itself

Maybe you have recognized it from the name, and this particular cartridge is a piece of the 'Light' collection. The Lite cartridges have immediately ended up being highly supported since their underlying uncovering. Not exclusively do a great deal of them fill in explicit cartridge topic holes inside the full cartridge gathering, but having unadulterated substance material and significantly less of the generally squandered additional items, they likewise make sense to be a mess progressively moderate.

The Lite Cupcake Wrappers cartridge was made for each cake (and particularly cupcake) dough punchers around. The round is packaged with 50 unique cupcake holders or wrapper pictures that you're ready to pick and remove to hold your newly prepared cupcake. The arrangement likewise offers a little decision of cupcake topper decorations, which are perfect for fixing off your definitive handcrafted cupcake.

You must love exactly how making every cupcake wrapper is presently so natural and fast, and the completed visual effect is cute. When you start to utilize this cartridge to adorn most of your handcrafted cupcakes, trust me, not simply will an old 'stripped' cake in a flash end up being amazingly uninteresting. Yet, you will search out chances to heat cakes for any event to get every one of the compliments from everyone that sees them.

The Designs and Sizes

Pictures for cupcake wrapper structures vacillate between fragile, for all intents and purposes doily looking examples to increasingly contemporary styles, alongside a few models that incorporate valuable words and expressions, so there is surely a unique format to suit each cupcake occasion.

One of the most constant inquiries in regards to this particular cartridge is concerning the size. The wrapper structures can be cut in size to oblige any size cupcake (sensibly speaking, obviously), yet be admonished that you may need to rehearse on more than one occasion before transforming into a specialist with what measurements your machine should be set to about the particular cupcake boundary. The uplifting news is you'll undoubtedly have the option to get the hang of it in a brief timeframe.

Undertaking Ideas

Normally, if you're just preparing a lot of cupcakes to expend yourself, you doubtlessly won't have any desire to utilize this cartridge. However, for each other event, it is, without a doubt, an unquestionable requirement to change over fundamental cupcakes into a touch of something unique. Loads of individuals utilize this specific cartridge to spruce up the standard cupcakes served at kids' parties. For social events, anyway, anyplace a cake or two is discovered, the Lite Cupcake Wrapper cartridge can make every one of them simply significantly more exceptional.

Tips on How to Ensure Its Longevity

First of all, ensure that you secure it consistently. When you are finished utilizing it, place a spread over your tangle. Clear plastic can support a major ordeal. On the off chance that you have two mats, you utilize both to cover each other from eye to eye. Likewise, clear out any abundance of paper that is deserted on the floor covering. You can do this by utilizing child wipes. In any case, if your Cricut mats have just exceeded their normal life regardless of genuine endeavors on your part to look after them, you can utilize a knitting splash to recover its stickiness.

Cartridges are an ongoing discussion among Cricut users for a variety of reasons.

A cartridge is what contains the images and fonts that you'll be cutting. Most cartridges hold 700 or 800 images. Lite cartridges contain about 50 images and have one or two creative features. Despite the limitations, you can still be creative and produce hundreds of variations with this less expensive choice.

You usually receive at least one cartridge with the purchase of your machine. Sometimes this is preloaded into your machine as a digital cartridge. You may buy downloadable digital cartridges online for immediate use, or you can buy the physical plastic cartridges that you slide into your machine.

When you purchase a cartridge, you can use that physical cartridge in your machine, or you also have the option to link that cartridge to the Cricut Craft Room (CCR).

The Craft Room allows you to view your images on your computer screen, making it easier to see and manipulate your projects.

By linking to CCR, you won't have to bother to switch out your cartridges physically. If you plan ever to sell the cartridges, then do not link them. Once they are linked, you are not legally allowed to sell them. This is understandable. Some people might link them to the Craft Room, so they have access to the images and then sell the physical cartridge.

To link your cartridges, you'll need to do the following. Load the cartridge you want to add to your machine. Go online to the Craft Room. Under all cartridges, select my cartridges. You will see a list of cartridges. Find the cartridge you want to add and click Link and follow the prompts.

Another advantage of adding your cartridges to the Craft Room is that you'll be able to pull images from several cartridges to use at one time. When you're using the physical cartridge, you can only use images from one cartridge at a time.

If you buy a used cartridge, you need to ask if it's linked. If it is, you will still be able to use the physical cartridge in your machine, but you will not be able to link it to the Craft Room. A cartridge can only be linked once. It is still possible to use the cartridge in the Craft Room, but you can't link it. You'll have to have the physical cartridge in your machine to cut the images.

It is now possible to purchase cartridges online and download them to your account. This means you don't have to wait for a physical cartridge to arrive in the mail. You have immediate access to the images. These are the digital cartridges that I referred to earlier.

Many people complain that the cartridges are too expensive. Instead of spending $80 on a cartridge with hundreds of images, many people would prefer to be able to buy an image they want for one dollar or two; that's where single images or sets come into play.

You can buy single digital images or smaller sets for a fraction of the cost of a full cartridge. You can even rent cartridge bundles for 30 days on a monthly subscription on the Cricut home page under the shopping section.

Make sure you take advantage of the free cartridges offered in the Craft Room. The only thing to remember is to finish your projects. Once the cartridge is no longer free, you will not be able to cut your image.

You can save money on cartridges watching for sales and special promotions.

It is possible to share physical cartridges with friends. This is good if they want a few images for a special project, but don't plan to use the cartridge enough to justify buying it.

Digital Handbooks for Easy Reference

Did you know you can download the digital handbook of any cartridge and save it as a PDF file on your computer? Just go to Cricut.com, click on the shop, images, and cartridges. Select any cartridge, click on it scrolling down the page till you see the link for the digital handbook, open it and save it to your hard drive for easy reference.

Sharing Cut Files

A cut file is a project that someone has already created and laid out on their Cricut. They saved the file and shared it on their blog or in the Craft Room. What this does is prevent you from re-creating the wheel.

If you see a project you like, you can save the file onto your computer. Then go to the Craft Room and import that file. You can then make the same cuts without having to figure out how to lay everything out. The images are already sized and laid out for you.

The advantage of this is you can save yourself a lot of time by using layouts that others have already created.

But here's the tricky part, you must already own the cartridges the images are from. You can't make the cuts if you don't own the cartridges the images originated from.

You can also save your projects and share them in the Craft Room for others to use.

When you see a cute project on Pinterest or a craft blog, you might want to ask if the cut file is available and, if so, what cartridges it uses.

Organization

If you're like most crafters, including me, you'll eventually become overrun with craft "stuff." You'll have paper stacks, vinyl rolls, and other material that you're planning to use someday spread all over your craft area.

Your cartridges may be lying around in a pile, and you have to spend twenty minutes searching every time you need a specific overlay or booklet.

Eventually, this creates such a feeling of chaos and frustration that you dread going into your Craft Room or crafting area.

This can all be solved with some organization. It may take you a few hours to get it all in order, but it will save you countless hours in the future. You'll no longer feel depressed every time you look at your crafting space.

Craft stores will often have storage containers specially made for certain types of crafts. But you may want to start at your local chain stores. They often have craft and office supply departments where you can find storage units cheaply.

You can find containers where you can sort all your paper into small shelves based on color and type of paper. If you don't like the ones at the craft store, then try an office supply store. If you live in an extremely humid area, you may want to store your paper in plastic containers.

Another option is to watch for garage sales that say "craft items." Many people spend hundreds of dollars getting set up for a particular craft and then discover they don't have the time or inclination to spend much time doing the craft. This can be a bonanza for other crafters.

Photo boxes can be used to keep your booklets and overlays safe and organized.

Some crafters copy their overlays, laminate them and bind them together on rings where they can easily be added or removed.

There are special carrying cases, binders, and totes designed just for cartridges.

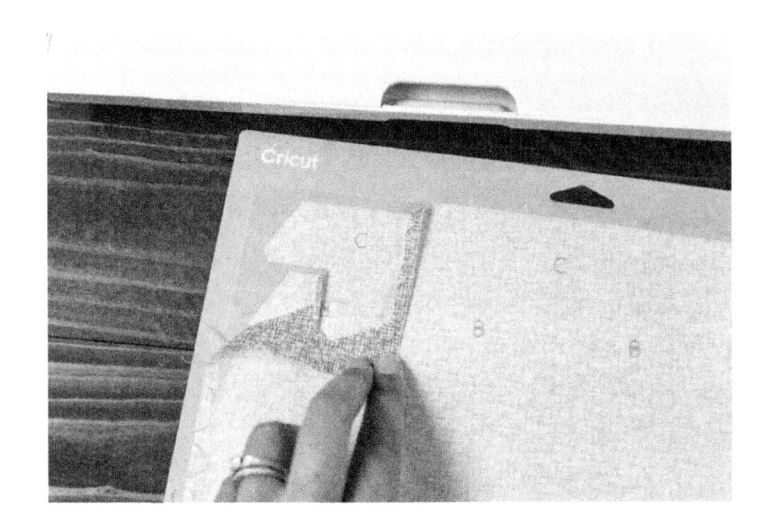

The first thing to remember is to make sure that you're using the right mat. The light grip ones are good for very light material, with the pink one being one of the strongest, and only to be used with the Cricut Maker. Once the design is cut, you'll probably be eager McBeaver about removing the project directly from the mat, but one of the problems with this is that often, the project will be ruined if you're not careful. Instead of pulling the project from the mat itself, bend the mat within your hand, and push it away from the project, since this will loosen it from the mat. Bend this both horizontally and vertically, so that the adhesive releases the project.

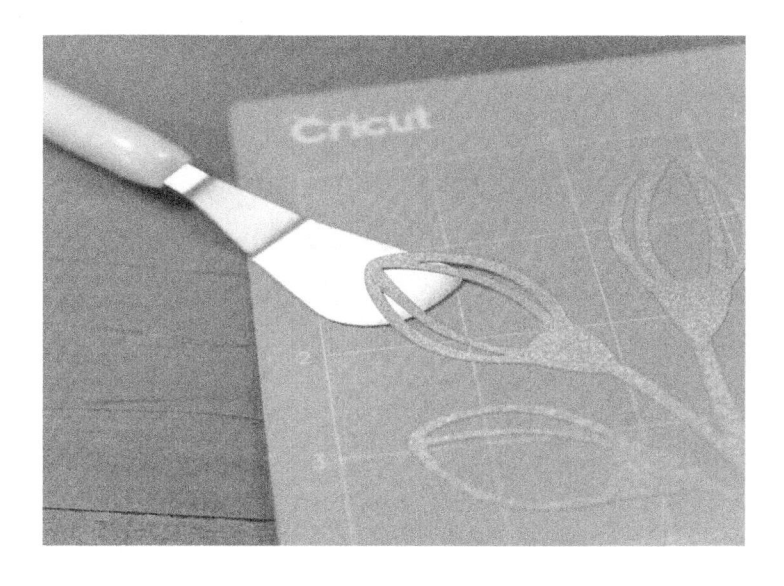

Do you remember the spatula tool that we told you to get with your Cricut machine early on? This is where you use it. Use this spatula to lightly pull on the vinyl, until you can grab it from the corner and lift it up. Otherwise, you risk curling it or tearing the mat, which is what we don't want.

Now, with the initial cuts, such as the paper ones, this will be incredibly easy. Trust me, I was surprised at how little effort it took, but one of the biggest things to remember is that with Cricut machines, you have to go slow when removing the material. Do this slowly, and don't get rushed near the end. Taking your time will save you a lot of problems, and it will even save you money and stress, too!

You will notice that Cricut mats are incredibly sticky, and if you don't have a Cricut spatula on hand or don't want to spend the money, metal spatulas will work too. You can put the paper on a flat surface and then lightly remove it. But always be careful when removing these items.

Cricut machines are pretty easy to use, and the beauty is that with the right understanding and ideas, you can make any items you want to.

Chapter 6: Maintenance of the Machine

The Cricut Cutter machine needs to be kept intact in a variety of ways: the blade must be replaced, the cutting mats must be taken care of, and the machine, in general, must be kept clean.

Cutting Blade

Every single blade you use might get up to fifteen thousand individual cuts before it needs to be replaced. To prolong this number of individual cuts, place the aluminum foil onto the cutting mat and cut out a few designs. This process keeps the blade extra sharp and lengthens the life of the blade. This number of cuts can be greatly based on the types of materials that have been cut by the blade. If you are doing many projects in which thick materials need to be cut, the blade will deteriorate quickly; the blade can also deteriorate quickly if you are cutting many materials under high pressure. A good way to know if your blade needs to be replaced is if the quality of your cuts starts to greatly decrease. If this happens, it's best to replace the cutting blade. When replacing the blade, it is always best to get blades that are Cricut brand. Generic blades are often not the best quality and will cause you to constantly replace your cutting blade. To install the new blade once, you've ordered the correct one, you need to first unplug your Cricut Cutter machine. Always unplug the machine before installing anything in your Cricut cutter. Next, you must remove the old, dull cutting blade from your Cricut Cutter machine. Once the cutting blade assembly has been separated, it is now time to eject the blade. Find the small silver button above the adjustment knob and press the button down; this will eject the cutting blade. Be very, very careful when doing this as the blade is extremely sharp and can easily cut through the skin. Keep all blades away from children and pets. To put in the new blade, insert the blade into the end of the blade assembly opposite the blade release button. The blade will then be pulled up into the assembly.

Subscribe to Cricut Access

If you really want to get a full range of use out of both your Cricut Explore machine as well as the Cricut Maker machine, we would recommend you subscribe to Cricut Access right away. There are two options for payment. You can either pay a monthly fee of $10, or you can pay once for the entire year. This works out to be slightly cheaper on a month-to-month basis. This will give you access to thousands of different predesigned projects as well as Cricut Access exclusive fonts, that you would otherwise have to pay to use. If you are planning to use your Cricut a lot, this will save you a lot of money as opposed to buying an image for every project individually. We can all agree it is a lot easier to pay one flat rate instead of having to figure out how much you are spending on projects. Get your money's worth out of your Cricut and subscribe to Cricut Access.

De-tack Your Cutting Mat

The Cricut Explore machine will come with a green 12"x12" standard grip cutting mat. The Cricut Maker machine will come with a blue light grip mat. As you already know, you will place your cutting material onto this mat before inserting it into the machine to cut. As you will come to find out, the green cutting mat is extremely sticky when it is brand new.

Keep Your Cutting Mat Covers

The cutting mats that you purchase for your projects will always come brand new with a plastic protecting sheet over them. This can be pulled off and put back on for the entire life of the mat. You will want to keep this plastic cover if you have the mat. It will keep the stickiness level up on your mat, and it will make the mat easier to store away when not in use.

Cutting Mat

The Cutting mat in addition to the cutting blade needs to be taken care of. One cutting mat can have a life of anywhere from twenty-five to forty cuts. The life of the cutting mat can vary from this amount depending on the pressure and speed at which the cuts have been made and the type of materials that have been cut on the mat. To prolong the life of your cutting mat, remove any debris from the mat after a cut and always avoid scraping the mat. If you scrape the mat, it can push any debris further into the mat. After each craft, it is best to run lukewarm water over the mat and dab it dry with a towel afterward. When a material can no longer adhere to the cutting mat, then it is time to finally replace the mat. It is recommended to get many cutting mats and rotate between them to prolong the life of all the cutting mats. This extends the life of the mats because one cutting mat will not be cut on for many, many projects in a small amount of time. It is also recommended that you keep all your cutting mats and all your cartridges and blades in a very organized manner. Throwing the components haphazardly can destroy and deteriorate them, so it is best to keep them in a very organized way. A benefit of keeping your Cricut Cutter components organized is that you won't lose or damage the very expensive items that are necessary for several projects.

How to Clean a Cricut Mat

Sometimes it also depends on the materials you use that make your machine dirty. For example, using felt means you'd need to grab stray pieces using tweezers. Another great way to clean your Cricut machine is to use a lint roller across the entire machine to pick up debris, scrap vinyl, and pieces of felt. You can also use this roller on your mats.

To clean your mats, if there is any leftover residue on your mats, the general rule is to use bleach and alcohol-free baby wipes to gently wipe the mat clean and remove it from grime, glue, and dust. You can also get yourself GOO GONE. Spray this on your mat and let it sit for 15 minutes, then use a scraper tool to remove the adhesive. But do this only if your mat is very dirty. Otherwise, wet wipes will do.

Another tip to keep your mats clean is by putting a protective cover back over them when you are not using them.

Cleaning the Cricut Machine

The final thing to keep clean is the actual Cricut Cutter machine. The machine needs to be wiped down with a damp cloth. Only wipe down the external panels of the machine and with the machine unplugged. Always wipe down the machine with a dry cloth after cleaning the outside of the machine. Never clean the Cricut

Cutter machine with abrasive cleaners such as acetone, benzene, and all other alcohol-based cleaners. Abrasive cleaning tools should also not be used on the Cricut Cutter machine. In addition, never submerge any component of the machine or the Cricut Cutter machine into the water, as it can damage the machine. Always keep the Cricut Cutter machine away from all foods, liquids, pets, and children. Keep the Cricut Cutter machine in a very dry and dust-free environment. Finally, do not put the Cricut Cutter machine in excessive heat, excessive cold, sunlight, or any area where the plastic or any other components on the Cricut Cutter machine can melt.

Ensure Your Machine Is on Stable Footing

This may seem pretty basic, but ensuring that your machine is on a level surface will allow it to make more precise cuts every single time. Rocking the machine or wobbling could cause unstable results in your projects.

Ensure no debris has gotten stuck under the feet of your machine that could cause instability before proceeding to the next troubleshooting step!

Redo all Cable Connections

So your connections are in the best possible working order, undo all your cable connections, blow into the ports or use canned air, and then securely plug everything back into the right ports. This will help to make sure all the connections are communicating with each other where they should be!

Completely Dust and Clean Your Machine

Your little Cricut works hard for you! Return the favor by making sure you're not allowing gunk, dust, grime, or debris to build up in the surfaces and crevices. Adhesive can build up on the machine around the mat input and on the rollers, so be sure to focus on those areas!

Check Your Blade Housing

Sometimes debris and leavings from your materials can build up inside the housings for your blades! Open them up and clear any built-up materials that could be impeding swiveling or motion.

Sharpen Your Blades

A very popular Cricut trick in use is to stick a clean, fresh piece of foil to your Cricut mat, and run it through with the blade you wish to sharpen. Running the blades through the thin metal helps to revitalize their edges and give them a little extra staying power until it's time to buy replacements.

Chapter 7: Tips and Tricks on How to Start and How to Make Your First Project

While Cricut's website offers many tips and techniques, there are some tried-and-true ways of using your machine and saving money and time.

10 Top Tips and Tactics for Success

1. Freezer paper is ideal for creating custom stencils.

2. Label blades for use on paper, vinyl, fabric, etc., only use those blades on that medium. It helps preserve the lifetime of the edges.

3. Learn the proper cutting methods and approved materials by reading the cutting guide on Cricut.com.

4. Spray paint is an excellent tool for coloring vinyl if you are ever in a hurry and do not have a required color on hand or the time for it to arrive.

5. Free fonts can be uploaded and used in the Cricut Design Space. Find free fonts on websites such as dafont.com, fontsquirrel.com, or 1001freefonts.com.

6. Personal images and pictures can be used for Cricut projects if the image is saved on the computer as a PNG, JPG, or SCG.

7. Test out materials before printing and cutting a final project to be sure it will work as planned.

8. Pens other than Cricut pens work with the machine. Some brands to try include Sharpie, American Crafts and Recollections.

9. Avoid paper curling by pulling the cutting mat from the project and not the other way around.

10. Lint rollers are great for removing leftover materials from cutting mats. If the carpets need further cleaning, use soap and water and gently rub clean with a soft cloth. Rinse with clean water and let air dry.

Cutting with Your Cricut

Masking tape or painter's tape is excellent to place on the edges of materials when they do not stick well to the cutting mat.

Thick cuts sometimes will not be cut completely. To avoid having to do it by hand, keep the material in place when it finishes cutting the first cut without pressing the arrows button to remove it and then cut it again by selecting the "Go" or "C" button.

Print and Cut

An inkjet printer works best for printing. A laser printer sometimes heats the toner too high, making it hard for the Cricut machine to read.

Internet Explorer or Safari is best for working with large images because these browsers support about 9 inches high and about 6 inches wide. Chrome and Firefox cap their heights around 8 inches tall and about 5 inches wide.

A white paper is best for printing the registration marks for projects. If the project is any other color, print and cut on white paper first, attach them to the colored paper before putting it into the Cricut.

Writing with Your Cricut

Pens work best when stored cap-side down. It keeps the ink at the tip.

Thin pens can have their barrel widened by winding tape around them. The electrical or painter's tape works well and does not leave a sticky residue behind.

Scoring with Your Cricut

Folding materials are made more comfortable using the scoring tool when placed in the machine's pen holder.

Deepen the score lines in a custom design by doubling up the canvas's score lines in the Design Space.

Embossing with Your Cricut

It can do! Use the accessory adapter in the place of the blade housing and insert the scoring stylus into it. When the Cricut tells of cutting, it will emboss instead.

Badges for Your Cricut

Sharpen blades with aluminum foil by cutting a basic design into the foil on the cutting mat.

Designing for Your Cricut

Firefox and Safari are best for using Design Space. Google Chrome does not work well with it.

Save the free designs that Design Space offers by saving a new project with the design and name it with a design description for easy access.

Cut the canvas exactly how it is laid out by selecting "All" and clicking on "Attach." It ensures everything stays where it is without the machine defaulting to individual cuts.

Instructional handbooks are available for Cricut Access members. This link is a functional place to learn how to assemble cartridges. (www.home.cricut.com/handbooks)

Cut the most massive layer last to avoid the material from moving around during the smaller cuts. It means placing the most massive layer as the topmost layer and the more delicate elements at the bottom in Design Space.

Chapter 8: FAQ for Cricut

What Is a Cricut?

A Cricut is a machine that you can use for cutting a variety of different art projects. It is a machine designed to speed up the crafting process and help you make professional and homemade crafts in the comfort of your own home.

Where Can I Download the Software for the Explore Machines?

You can go to design.cricut.com and use your Cricut ID to log in. This process is relatively easy and anyone comfortable enough to download things from the computer will be able to do this. Even if you have never downloaded anything before, the website will prompt you to download Design Space and everything after that will be guided as well.

Where Can I Download the Software If I Am on Mobile?

If you are on iOS, you have to go to the App Store and search for the Cricut Design Space app. If you are on Android, simply go to Google Play and search for the same thing. All you have to do is download it like any other app, log in, and you are ready to use Design Space.

What Are the Differences between the Machines?

The Cricut Explore 1 does not have Bluetooth and will need a Cricut Wireless Bluetooth Adapter to use with your mobile. The Cricut Maker, Explore Air and Explore Air 2 all have built-in Bluetooth.

The Cricut Explore 1 also has a single Carriage, which means that it cannot multitask like the Explore Air, Cricut Maker, and Explore Air 2.

The Explore Air 2 comes in different colors and cuts faster than the Explore Air and the Cricut Explore 1.

Cricut Maker has storage space and can cut through thicker materials.

Does My Machine Come with a Carry Bag of Sorts?

No, it does not. A carry bag can be purchased from the store, but it is incredibly overpriced. What's the use of having a Cricut if you can't make your own carry bag?

Writing and Scoring, Can I Do It?

Yes, you can. With the Cricut Maker, Explore Air and Explore Air 2, you can either write and cut or score and cut at the same time. The Cricut Explore 1 can do all of it too, but not at the same time.

Is the Design Space the Same for Both the Cricut Maker and the Explore?

Yes, it is. Long story short; it is exactly the same.

Does the Cricut Maker Have Fast Mode?

Yes, it does. It has a setting for up to 2x faster than normal.

What Is the Thickest My Cutting Materials Can Be for the Cricut Explore Machines?

The Explore machines can cut materials up to 2mm, but nothing thicker.

What Is the Thickest My Cutting Materials Can Be for the Cricut Maker?

The Cricut Maker can cut materials up to 2.5mm, which doesn't sound like much, but it makes a huge difference.

Do I Need the Internet?

Yes and no. When you are on a desktop, there is no offline option for Design Space. However, if you are on mobile, the app will allow you to work offline and you won't need the Internet for any of it.

Can Design Space Work on More Than One Device?

Yes. Design Space works with the cloud and not a specific device. This means that anything with access to the cloud can access your account and use your Cricut machine without any hassle.

How Long Do Images I Have Purchased Stay in My Possession?

Images do not expire once you have purchased them. They stay yours forever.

Why Is My Material Tearing All the Time and What Can I Do to Stop It?

There are many reasons why your materials might be tearing. It could be that you are not using the right settings, your blade is too blunt, the design that you are trying to cut is too intricate and you need to make it larger or cut slower. There are more possibilities, though. You could be using the wrong blade for your crafts or your materials just aren't working well enough with your Cricut Maker and you might want to invest in better materials in the future. Your mat may also be too sticky or too loose.

Are My Old Blades Compatible with the Cricut Maker?

Yes, they are. The Cricut Maker is compatible with old accessories and tools, as well as new ones that will be released in the future.

How Do I Change the Blades and Accessories?

For the blades, you can merely open the clamp marked with a B and remove the blade housing. Now you have an empty clamp and you won't be able to do anything without another blade in the clamp.

To replace the blade in the housing, all you have to do is remove the blade carefully so you don't cut yourself, remove the protective cover from the new blade, and put that in the new housing just like the one you took out. There is a magnet in the housing that keeps the blades in place. All that's left is to return the housing to the clamp and you will be ready to go.

For the accessories, you want to open the clamp and slide the accessory adapter out. Do this by pushing it upward from below. Add your accessory and put it back in the clamp.

The Cricut Explore 1 only has one clamp, which means you will have to switch between the accessory adapter and blade housing. It changes nothing about the process of replacing the blades and accessories. The only difference is that both use the same clamp.

Do I Need a Printer to Use My Cricut?

In a word, no. Using your Cricut doesn't require ink from a printer, though there are some materials on the market for Cricut, which are specifically meant to be printed on before using.

If you're not using these items, then you will find that you can get the most out of your machine without that feature.

If you wish to print things then cut them, this is known as the Print then Cut method and there is a wealth of knowledge about this on the internet. You can make iron-on decals, tattoos, and so much more!

Chapter 9: Cricut Dictionary

When working with the Cricut cutting machines and Design Space, you are going to come across different terminology. The following is a glossary of the Cricut vocabulary to help you better understand the system. The following are general Cricut terminology as "Design Space" terminology.

Backing

The backing is the back sheet of a material such as vinyl. It is the part of the material that gets stuck onto the cutting mat and is usually the last part of the material to be removed after cutting, weeding, and transfer of the project.

Bleed

The bleed refers to a space around each item to be cut. This gives the cutting machine the ability to make a more precise cut. It is a small border that separates cutting items on a page. This option can be turned off, but it is not recommended.

Bonded Fabric

Bonded fabric is a material that is not very elastic, it is held together with adhesive and is not typical woven type fabric.

If there is some gunk visible on the blade, pinch around the blade shaft using a very careful grip with your opposite thumb and forefinger, and bring it back, making sure you don't go against the blade angle as you do. This will remove any foreign material from your blade tip and make your cuts more accurate.

You may also take a ball of tin foil and poke the blade a few times into the cup, which will remove debris while also allowing a minor sharpening on them.

Blade

Cricut has a few different types of cutting blades and tips. Each blade has its own unique function enabling it to cut various materials.

Blade Housing

The blade housing is the cylindrical tube that holds the blade and fits into the blade head and blade accessory compartment of the Cricut cutting machine.

Blank

Cricut offers items, called blanks, to use with various projects for vinyl, iron-on, heat transfer vinyl, or infusible ink. These items include T-shirts, tote bags, coasters, and baby noisiest.

Brayer

The Brayer is a tool that looks a bit like a lint roller brush. It is used to flatten and stick material or objects down smoothly as it irons out bubbles, creases, etc.

Bright Pad

A Bright Pad is a device that looks like a tablet. This device has a strong backlight to light up materials to help with weeding and defining intricate cuts. It is a very handy tool to have and can be used for other DIY projects as well.

Butcher Paper

Butcher paper is the white paper that comes with the Cricut Infusible Inks sheets. It is used to act as a barrier between the EasyPress or iron when transferring the ink sheet onto a blank or item.

Carriage

The carriage is the bar in the Cricut cutting machine through which the blade moves.

Cartridge

Cartridges are what the older models of the Cricut cutting machine used to cut images. Each cartridge would hold a set of images. They can still be used with the Cricut Explore Air 2, which has a docking site for them. If you want to use them with a Cricut Maker, you will have to buy a USB adapter. Design Space still supports the use of Cartridge images.

Cartridges also come in a digital format.

Cricut Maker Adaptive Tool System

The Cricut Maker comes with an advanced tools system control using intricate brass gears. These new tools have been designed to aid the machine in making precise cuts and being able to cut more materials such as wood, metal, and leather.

Cut Lines

These are the lines along which the cutting machine will cut out the project's shapes.

Cutting Mat

There are a few different types of cutting mats also known as machine mats. Most of the large mats can be used on both the Cricut Explore Air 2 and the Cricut Maker. The Cricut Joy needs mats that are designed specifically for it.

Cut Screen

When you are creating projects in Design Space, there is a green button on the top right-hand corner of the screen called the Make it button. When the project is ready to be cut, this button is clicked on. Once that button has been clicked, the user is taken to another screen where they will see how the project is going to be cut out. This is the Cut Screen.

Drive Housing

The Drive Housing is different from Blade Housing in that it has a gold wheel at the top of the blade. These blades can only be used with the Cricut Maker cutting machine.

EasyPress

A Cricut EasyPress is a handheld pressing iron that is used for iron-on, heat transfer vinyl (HTV), and infusible ink. EasyPress's latest models are the EasyPress 2 and the EasyPress Mini.

EasyPress Mat

There are a few different EasyPress Mat sizes that are available on the market. These mats make transferring iron-on, heat transfer vinyl, and infusible ink a lot simpler. These mats should be used for these applications instead of an ironing board to ensure the project's success.

Firmware

Firmware is a software patch, update or newly added functionality for a device. For cutting machines, it would be new driver's updates, cutting functionality, and so on.

Both Design Space software on Cricut cutting machines and Cricut EasyPress 2 machines need to have their Firmware updated on a regular basis.

Go Button

This can also be called the "Cut" button. This is the button on the Cricut cutting or EasyPress machine that has the green Cricut "C" on it. It is the button that is pressed when a project is ready to be cut or pressed for the EasyPress models.

JPG File

A JPG file is a common form of digital image. These image files can be uploaded for use with a Design Space project.

Kiss Cut

When the cutting machine cuts through the material but not the material backing sheet, it is called a Kiss Cut.

Libraries

Libraries are lists of images, fonts, or projects that have been uploaded by the user or maintained by Cricut Design Space.

PNG File

A PNG file is another form of a graphics (image) file. It is most commonly used in Web-based graphics for line drawings, small graphic/icon images, and text.

Ready to Make Projects

Design Space contains ready-to-make projects that are projects that have already been designed. All the user has to do is choose the project to load in Design Space, get the material ready, and then make it to cut the design out. These projects can be customized as well.

Scraper Tool

The Scraper tool comes in small and large. It is used to make sure the material sticks firmly to a cutting mat, object, or transfer sheet.

Self-Healing Mat

Cricut has many handy accessories and tools to help with a person's crafting. One of these handy tools is the Self-Healing Mat. This mat is not for use in a cutting machine but can be used with handheld slicing tools to cut material to exact specifications

SVG File

The SVG file format is the most common format for graphic files in Cricut Design Space. This is because these files can be manipulated without losing their quality.

Transfer Sheet/Paper

A transfer sheet or transfer paper is a sheet that is usually clear and has a sticky side. These sheets are used to transfer various materials like transfer vinyl, sticker sheets, and so on to an item.

Weeding/Reverse Weeding

Weeding is the process of removing vinyl or material from a cut pattern or design that has been left behind after removing the excess material. For example, weeding the middle of the letter "O" to leave the middle of it hollow.

Reverse Weeding would be leaving the middle of the letter "O" behind and removing the outside of it.

Weeding Tool

The weeding tool has a small hooked head with a sharp point. This tool is used to pick off the material that is not needed on a cut. For instance, when cutting out the letter 'O,' the weeding tool is used to remove the middle of the letter so that it is hollow. Cleaning up a cut design with the Weeding tool is called weeding.

Conclusion

Congratulations on making it to the end. We hope that the chapters in this book have helped you get more familiar with your Cricut machine or that it has persuaded you to get one for the first time. There are so many amazing things that you can do with a Cricut machine. This book is only the beginning of what your creativity can get you if you work with the Cricut machine. There are only new and better updates that are happening to the machine, so now is the best time to get one and get in the door to understanding what it can do for you. We hope that the information we have provided you on what materials you can use with the machine, how to get your first project started, and all the project ideas are the tools you need to achieve the goals that you have with the Cricut machine.

The next step is to put what you have learned from this book into practice. Keep this book handy as you start out working with your Cricut machine so that you always have a quick reference guide with you. This is a great way for you to get to know the machine and not waste any time or material when you are just starting out. You can also remember that this book helps you through figuring out any problems you might face with the Design Space software or remembering any of the common mistakes that Cricut users can make with bad cuts. You should be well equipped to make all of the projects of your dreams and you are well on your way to impressing your friends and family with your newly acquired skill of homemade gifts and décor. You should also take the time to consider selling your projects to make a profit. You can have a really good side business in no time that can help you not only pay for the machine and the materials you are using, but also put some extra money in your pocket to pay your bills or get extra holiday gifts as well. There are many bonuses to getting a Cricut machine and we hope you have the opportunity to discover them all.

Happy crafting!